CHICAGO HOUSES

BY JANET BAILEY

PHOTOGRAPHY BY JONAS DOVYDENAS

St. Martin's Press
New York

Library of Congress Cataloging in Publication Data

Bailey, Janet.
  Chicago houses.

  1. Architecture, Domestic—Illinois—Chicago.
2. Chicago (Ill.)—Dwellings. I. Title.
NA7238.C4B3 728.8'3'0977311   81-5685
ISBN 0-312-13179-8   AACR2

Printed in Hong Kong by The South China Printing Co.

Book Design by R.J. Luzzi

FOR DON AND REBECCA BARLIANT

PREFACE

Sometimes the best houses come into existence without even an architectural midwife. Certainly the 19th century American vernacular styles, such as Samuel Sloan's, using only "copybook" methods are testimony to this.

Now here comes a tidy, well-bred book about Chicago houses. The majority included here are examples of "vernacular" types (Italianate, Romanesque, Victorian, Tudor, Gothic, Georgian, Colonial) and, because of this, the Wrightian, Prairie School image of Chicago is, for me, definitely enriched. It is a simplistic supposition that Chicago architecture is a coin with only two sides—Mies/commercial and Wright/residential. Thankfully, this notion has been eroded as less well-known and often less talented architects surface to flush out Chicago's very rich architectural condition.

On the commercial side of the coin, the side of the "big shoulders," the often dogmatic Mies van der Rohe image has been long since embellished by wonderfully eccentric figures such as Andrew Rebari, Harry Weese, Bertrand Goldberg, and Walter Netsch. On the residential side, the image of the powerful Wright is now seen as but only one view of "the American house." In Chicago, there are now alternative architectural visions, such as those of Howard Van Doren Shaw (unfortunately absent here), David Adler, Boyd Hill, George Fred Keck, and Edward Dart. Not always demonstrating precise lineage, these often disparate figures nonetheless round out Chicago's high-art image.

At least as important, however, is Chicago's architectural tradition which, like the rest of American "copybook" history, transmuted the stylized models of Europe into useful residential forms for America. In Chicago, these forms are further synthesized by the powerful Prairie Style of turn-of-the-century architects determined to break out of the European box: four-square, aristocratic, and bilaterally symmetrical.

Thus, the merging of a very special American vernacular tradition, in combination with some of its architectural antecedents, is one of the central values of this book. That even a powerfully influential city such as Chicago can define its architectural heritage as something quite beyond the one dimensional view of its often overly pragmatic position is helped by this and other recent publications that reinforce the view that Chicago is far richer in its architecture than has been previously supposed.

STANLEY TIGERMAN

TABLE OF CONTENTS

INTRODUCTION

Looking at houses is a pastime available to everyone. A Sunday drive or evening stroll through hometown neighborhoods accommodates our perpetual curiosity about the way other people live. Looking at a house, we measure its character against our own standards and tastes. We inhabit the rooms in our imagination, trying to feel the fit of them.

But there is another way to see a house. We can view it as an object—a piece of work that, beautiful or clumsy, has an individual history and discernible reasons for having that sort of domed roof or this kind of curving staircase. And we can look at it as a small part of a much larger story: the growth of the town and the architecture which shaped it.

Chicago's architecture is particularly rich and distinctive. The city's life story is written in its buildings and even the most offhanded observer can learn to read it. From the raucous trading pits of the Board of Trade to the glittering stores on Michigan Avenue, Chicago is animated by the push and pull of big money and labyrinthine politics. The very center of the city is all business. In the 1880's the world's first skyscraper was built there and downtown has been pushing ever since. Close in to the north, homes for the wealthy and commercial buildings cluster together. Miles of parkland curve around Lake Michigan—the city's front lawn. Deeper into the city are the neighborhoods—Greek, Italian, Polish, German, Chinese, Black, and lots more, each with a history as distinct and complex as a separate town. Beyond the neighborhoods, radiating out to the north, west and south are the suburbs, joined to the city by long ribbons of rail-lines and expressways.

The sample of Chicago's houses in this book illustrates how people in this sprawling city are putting to use 100 years of residential architecture. By examining each house, we also glimpse Chicago's past and begin to understand its special place in a century of architectural change.

The simplest way to start looking at a house for its history is to fit it into a category and then to see just how alike or different it is compared to the other members of the category. Classifying houses in Chicago, it turns out, is a lot easier because of the Great Fire of 1871. Chicago's first major contribution to architecture had been the invention of balloon-frame construction in the 1830's. This was a method of putting together wooden buildings quickly and economically, but these wooden houses were the tinder that ignited and spread the Chicago Fire. By 1871, so many thousands of these wood frame structures were clustered together in all parts of the city that one small, uncontrolled fire kindled the first block and that block kindled the next until, after four days of burning, Chicago was virtually leveled. Except for the survivors of the fire, such as the one on page 9 (Northside Frame), all of Chicago's houses can be placed within those architectural categories that have developed since the late nineteenth century.

Eastern cities have uninterrupted lines of tradition that date from the earliest colonies. In the Southwest, the customs of American Indians and seventeenth century Spanish settlers have shaped the towns. In Chicago, the slate was wiped clean. The business of the city after the fire was to build. Architects and engineers came to Chicago in great numbers. They planted new kinds of buildings in its marshy ground. They shaped new ideas and new materials into a style that would change America's landscape.

William LeBaron Jenny, Louis Sullivan, John Wellborn Root, Daniel Burnham, their associates and contemporaries began to practice a kind of architecture which went far beyond simply drafting a design to be handed over to a builder. They mastered new techniques such as steel frame construction that made the world's first skyscraper possible. The architect's firm became an association of specialists in design, engineering foundation-building, fire protection and interior ornamentation. Every step of planning and construction was controlled by a single vision. Instead of patterning a building to suit a ponderous historical style with Greek columns or Roman arches, the new architects drew up cleaner, more simplified designs governed more by their real human uses. The practical demands of economy and efficiency were balanced against the need for comfort and pleasure. Light, airy and open spaces—these were all part of the character of the Chicago School of Architecture.

But traditional building styles did not yield either quickly or quietly to these innovations. If they had, Chicago's houses would present an orderly progression of sensible designs advancing into the middle of the twentieth century. The reality is quite different. The years of Chicago's rebirth provided a foundation for the architecture of the future, but they also coincided with the most exuberant trends of the Victorian Age. Toward the end of the 1880's, the more restrained style of earlier years were supplanted by romantic, heady mixtures that succeeded or failed with equally unselfconscious zest. The vocabulary of buildings included grand Greek columns and ornate Gothic spires. The architect could choose between the formal balance of Georgian facades or the magnificent asymmetry of the French chateau.

The catchall category of Chicago houses that includes the most flamboyant is called "Queen Anne." Dwellings as different as the row house on page 46 and the brown brick pastiche on page 76 go by this name. Ornate and asymmetrical, Queen Anne houses have towers, chimneys and lacy woodwork poking out from every angle. The style follows no rules, allowing an unparalleled degree of eccentricity. This Victorian gingerbread was maligned and rejected for years, but has recently regained its respectability. Queen Annes are being bought up and restored all over the city and suburbs.

Another common Chicago type is the Italianate house. Among the first designs to satisfy the Victorian nostalgia for historic styles, Italianate ornaments were applied on all kinds of residential and commercial buildings. The houses on page 22 and page 28 were enthusiastically adopted in Chicago. Henry Hobson Richardson forged this robust style from a number of historic elements, but with results entirely different from the eclecticism of Queen Anne. The authentic character of the masonry and the cohesiveness of the plans were to influence the work of Louis Sullivan and Frank Lloyd Wright.

While these and other historic motifs were freely adapted for the turn-of-the-century house, Revival architecture was also taking hold. The idea of Revivalism was to recreate precisely and purely the classic buildings of the past. Architects imitated Tuscan villas or medieval European castles in great detail. They brought new life to the strong simplicity of Early American designs. The house on page 65 is an example of Italianate Revival. The powerful appeal of these historic styles persisted well into the twentieth century. The chateau on page 156 and the Georgian mansion on page 166 were both built in the 1930's.

This picturesque range of architectural styles was shared by many Eastern and Midwestern cities. But Chicago's peculiar history was to produce, at the hands of Frank Lloyd Wright and his followers, the first truly new, truly indigenous domestic architecture in America. His predecessors were Jenny and Sullivan, from whom he learned to appreciate the value of human scale and to discard confining historic precedents. His totally original "Prairie Houses" conformed to the flat contours of Chicago's landscape. Wright shaped wood, brick and stone in ways consistent with their own nature rather than forcing them into the intricate forms of century-old styles.

The Prairie house like the one on page 122 was the very first to break away completely from the conventions of historic architecture, yet it existed quiescently beside the traditional house for many years before its enormous influence was felt. Meanwhile, the remarkable inventiveness of Wright's ideas played a large part in the growth of the International Style, a European architecture introduced into the United States in the 1930's. Constructed with hardedged products of the Machine Age, this style matured into the functional geometry of mid-twentieth century architecture. The austere glass and steel houses on pages 214 and 178 are both descendants of the International Style.

Certainly not every house in Chicago, nor even every house in this book, fits neatly into one or the other of these categories. The Second Empire house on page 38 is a Victorian modeled after an earlier French style. The contemporary houses on page 196 and page 203 are only very remotely connected to the modernism of the International Style. In the city itself there are sturdy brick bungalows, Gothic cottages, Shingle Style houses with their unique wood siding and more.

But the houses in this book were not chosen to retell the history of the city or the development of its architecture. They are here because their strong personalities, individual aesthetics and remarkable diversity admirably represent the best in Chicago houses.

Northside Frame-1830's

The balloon-frame system of construction was invented in Chicago in the 1830's. Because the method required little wood and few skills, it made it possible for a couple of people to nail together a house very quickly. Soon, frontier towns all the way to San Francisco mushroomed with balloon-frame structures similar to the two-and-a-half story house pictured here on the north side of the city. But in Chicago 40 years of building burned to ashes in one night in the Great Fire of 1871. This house is one of the very few that survived.

Its simple facade has been restored to its original proportions, based on early photographs tracked down by the owners. The rectangular windows are of modern design, but duplicate the size and placement of the originals. Untouched are the Italianate paired brackets that adorn the gabled roof.

The interior of the house is emphatically contemporary. The architect who redesigned it, Marvin Uhlman, began by gutting it top to bottom. He started over by plunging a skylighted stairwell down the center of the house. The front door leads into an alcove partly defined by a contoured wall, enclosing a powder room, that projects into the main living area from the right. To the left, an almost free-standing closet echoes the elliptical shape of the powder room. The living room centers around a fireplace. The open space follows the curve of the right hand wall and forms the dining room. Various details of design increase the illusion of a larger space.

9

Uninterrupted strips of oak flooring lie at an angle, binding the living room and dining area together. White walls and light natural fabrics also play a part in the continuity of space.

At the back of the main floor, there are a kitchen and a playroom with sliding glass doors leading onto a deck. The playroom connects to the kitchen and shares its rubber tile flooring. The room serves as a natural entryway from the backyard and is impervious to muddy boots.

The master bedroom occupies the entire front part of the second floor. Two children's rooms are at the rear. The only exceptions to the utter simplicity of the decor are the warmly colored fairy tale murals in the baby's room.

The basement of the house is sufficiently above ground to allow for fairly large windows, which bring light into a study, a maid's room and a laundry.

The distinctive character of this house comes first from the contrast between its traditional facade and the severe simplicity of the interior; and from the smooth and pleasing connection between its horizontal and vertical spaces.

Built-in closets and drawers run along the wall opposite the windows in the master bedroom. The pink pillows are the only accents in a subdued and beautiful room.

Natural and artificial light work to effect with the help of a mirrored wall in the master bathroom.

A minimum of clutter and plenty of storage space are the keynotes here.

A sunny deck off the playroom is a good place for children (and dogs).

Black rubber tile flooring and sleek black appliances give style to an all-white kitchen.

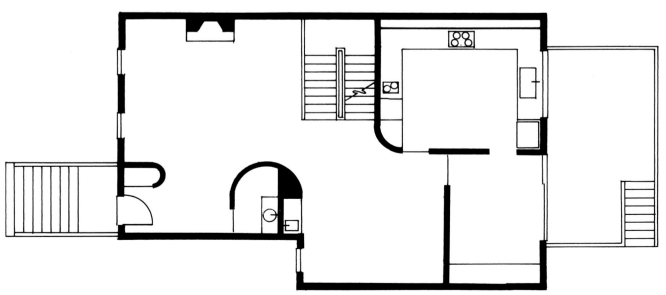

Surburban Italianate-1854

his graceful clapboard Victorian in one of Chicago's oldest northern suburbs began as a one-room tannery in 1854. Over the next 80 years it has patiently supported many changes, beginning with the first owner's decision to move in and live there. Since the tannery was made with balloon-frame construction (see Northside Frame, page 9) he easily raised the original structure, built a new ground floor beneath it and added a wing at that level. Wood was scarce and this first remodeling saved a perfectly good roof.

The sturdy little frame cottage soon changed hands. In 1869, its new owner added the features which make the house Italianate, a much admired architectural style at the time. He put up the ornamental cornice and brackets under the eaves. He also added two bays, one on the front, the other on the left side of the house, facing south, with tall arched windows that are also characteristically Italianate. At the same time, he built a kitchen behind the living room.

Two years later, the whole house was moved to its present site, then part of the owner's farm. A full basement at the new location raised the first floor above ground level. A second wing, longer than the first, was added at the right side of the house. A porch was added to this wing in 1904. Since then, the house has been left in peace.

Many, perhaps even most, 100-year-old houses in the Chicago area have similar patchwork pasts. Their porches torn down, windows bricked up, new walls erected, these houses have been reshaped by every hand that has held the deed.

Not surprisingly, the house tends to ramble out from the center stairway, reflecting the history of its growth. To the left as you enter the hallway is a den with a bay at the far end. To the right is the living room that has a bay at the front end, and opposite that a fireplace. The arrangement of antiques and reproductions in the room, and in the dining room behind it, suggests the elegance of an old Southern mansion. A cozy study, fronted by the porch on the right side of the house, adjoins the living room at one end. The sunny first floor of the south wing, on the left side of the house, is used as a family room, a place where grandchildren can swarm and drip jelly on the carpet.

The upstairs is given over to bedrooms—two in the center of the house and one over each wing.

A succession of craftsmen, over a stretch of 50 years, have pieced together this remarkably handsome house that has the balanced proportions of the purest and most deliberate Italianate architecture.

Westside Vernacular-1858

Built in 1858 in a western suburb of the city, this simple rectangular house, with its steep gable roof in the form of an inverted V, is almost a symbol for the word house. Its balloon frame construction (see page 9) is an example of vernacular architecture at its best.

Certain elements in the decoration belong to the Italianate style; for instance, the tall, round-headed windows on the first floor with their hood molds. This arch motif is carried out in the large fanlight and curved canopy over the front door. The broad band at the eaves accentuates the roof line and works with the vertical cornerboards to frame the whole facade.

However pleasing the original exterior, the interior posed certain problems with its unimaginative arrangement of tight, box-like rooms.

Improvements on the original plan began soon after the house was built, when it was moved to its present site. The first additions were a new dining room and kitchen. The current owners, who bought the house in the 1940's, enclosed the space above the addition to make a master bedroom and converted the living room into one room.

For all these structural additions and changes, it is really the decor of the house which compensates for the inadequacies of size and layout. Every room on the first floor is painted and carpeted in a rich yellow, creating a continuous flow from room to room. The problem of a long and very narrow living room has been solved by the arrangement of the furniture.

The owners have a varied collection of antiques that have come to them from both sides of their family which add much to the character of the rooms.

The outside of the house has a delightful simplicity; its rooms have a sunny charm. It is altogether a very appealing example of what can be achieved inside the walls of an unpretentious frame house.

Above the wainscotting in the dining room,
the walls have been hand-stenciled by
the owners. They designed the border
themselves, then copied a design by Moses
Eaton, the mid-eighteenth-century stenciler,
for the larger pattern.

The old-fashioned design of the wallpaper, repeated in the fabric of the curtains and on the bolsters on the beds, gives a sense of unity to this inviting bedroom.

An old rocker and a window seat under a broad window get together to form a comfortable retreat.

Greenhouse Kitchen-1870's

The Italianate style of architecture became popular during the Civil War and because of its great adaptability survived the tides of changing fashion until the end of the nineteenth century. The style has many variations (see Grande Dame, p.106 and Suburban Italianate, p.18) but always present are such features as a flat or low-pitched roof, deep eaves with ornamental brackets and tall, arched windows. The Italianate building is usually in the shape of a rectangle, two or three stories high.

This house, which has managed to keep its integrity through several alterations over the years, stands on the north side of the city. It was built in the 1870's, soon after the Fire. The formal balance of its smooth brick facade is almost obscured by the aggressive sweep of the curving veranda. This porch, with its Tuscan columns, and the stacked bays, with their rounded-off Italianate windows, on the right side of the house are Victorian additions that somewhat overshadow the original symmetry of the style.

Around 1888, a new wing was added to the back of the house which included a full glassed-in greenhouse. At the same time, the dining room and kitchen were relocated upstairs in what is now the main level. The greenhouse was originally separate from the dining room and kitchen but the current owners remodeled the space to make one large, square kitchen that is the focal point of the house.

The front of the house on this level still holds to a typical Victorian arrangement of rooms. To the right of the hall are the living room and behind that the parlor, with its bay window. An open shelf unit at the end of the hall gives a view into the kitchen from the front rooms. The greenhouse is visible through a window to the right of the marble fireplace in the parlor. Although the front rooms are somewhat narrow,

their high ceilings and tall windows create a sense of openness and space.

On the second floor, the master bedroom and a sitting room were included in the original floor plan. The two smaller bedrooms are part of the wing that was added later.

The third floor consists of one big raftered family room with open shelving for books and games and built-in benches piled with cushions.

A few years after this house was built, residential architects became more academically exact in recreating historic styles. For instance, the house on p.106 (Grande Dame) was built late in the 1890's and its materials, ornaments and floor plan are all more precisely a copy of the classic Italianate model. This house, on the other hand, is a nice example of an adaptation of the style that still has a strong identity of its own.

The lofty windows behind the sofa form a dramatic background to this end of the living room. This room, and the parlor beyond it, share the beauty and rarity of bird's eye maple floors with a mixed hardwood parquet border.

Landmark Restoration-1883

T his gently imposing stone house, and its surrounding neighborhood could serve as a textbook illustration of urban renewal.

The area was developed soon after Chicago's fire. It soon became fashionable and both mansions and smaller homes were built here between 1873 and 1900. But the neighborhood began to deteriorate. Early in the 1900's, some of these single family dwellings had already been converted to rooming houses. By the 1960's, the neighborhood had decayed so disastrously that the city began to demolish whole blocks and clear them for future use. In the early 1970's, only four blocks of houses remained,

isolated inside a perimeter of empty land. Working together as a group, five prospective buyers approached the city, which agreed to salvage the neighborhood. On the same day, they all purchased houses in the area. Two years later, the neighborhood was designated a Chicago landmark. As the restoration of the houses has continued, the value of the property has increased astronomically.

The street where this house stands is an architectural sampler of the most popular styles of the late nineteenth century: Italianate, Queen Anne, Romanesque and, as with this house, Second Empire, a style which originated during the reign of Napoleon III. The most distinctive element of this style is the mansard roof. This particular house has a straight-sided mansard roof, but other mansards may have either convex or concave sides for a more ornate effect. The dormer in the steeply sloping roof is typical of the Second Empire, as is the bracketed metal cornice at the eaves.

When the owner moved into the house the plumbing in all seven bathrooms worked, the mantels were intact and even the tooled leather wainscotting in the front hall was undamaged. But the job of restoration was still enormous and the owner has done it entirely on his own. He began by fixing up the two apartments on the property—one in the basement of the main house and one in the coach house.

Fortunately for the owners, ornamental details, such as this graceful ceiling molding and the stained glass inset over the door at the right, have not been destroyed over the years.

A wide arched molding sets apart a sleeping alcove from the rest of the room.

Dominating the kitchen is the attractive arched brick recess that houses the stove.

A striking view from the back of the house to the front bay of the living room.

All the original
mantels, like this
handsome one in
stone, have mirac-
ulously survived
intact.

Every room in the main house has been repaired and restored with scavenged pieces and handcraftsmanship. For example, the greenhouse that projects from the back of the coach house was built with sections of curved plate glass that were part of a display case at Marshall Field before the store was remodeled. The owner bought the glass inexpensively and made the brass strips that hold it in place.

Because of the months of full-time labor that were invested in the house and the community effort to preserve the neighborhood, a hopeless piece of real estate has become a gracious, livable, highly valued home.

Victorian Row House
cir. 1888

This Victorian gabled house is one of a row in a landmark district close to the center of the city. Several rows back up one to another here, and the shared back yards heighten the quality of neighborhood created by the uniform facades.

These rows were designed during the 1880's and 1890's by the firm of A.M.F. Colton and Son. They were built as rental units by a religious institution that needed a good investment. In 1974, the tenants formed an association and bought them outright.

The houses are raised above street level on high foundations because in

any areas of Chicago the basements ould not be sunk too deep into the ity's sandy soil: the high water table ould cause bad seepage problems.

The rows are built of red brick in a ery pared-down Queen Anne style. Details of decoration vary: some have ables and dormers, others have hansard roofs and even an occasional urret. The doorways are slightly re- essed under brick arches, a form hat is frequently repeated over the vindows. Although the different rows vere built over a 20-year period, their ariety of detail is outweighed by their eneral consistency of style.

This three-story house, built in the ate 1880's, when families were big, has even bedrooms. Since the present wners bought it, a great deal of repair nd restoration has gone into it. They ave stripped all the wood work, refin-

ished floors, installed a marble floor in the foyer, replastered extensively, remodeled the bathrooms and kitchen and removed the back porch for an unobstructed view of the back yard.

The floor plan is notable because it is so common both to row houses and to other inner city houses built in these decades. The entry opens onto a stairway which occupies one side of a hallway leading to the back of the house. Off the hall is the living room, sometimes, (but not in this case), a parlor, then the dining room. The hall leads into the kitchen and pantry. Behind them are the back stairs. Bed- rooms and baths are all on the upper floors.

The owners' use of Victorian antiques with contemporary furniture harmon- izes well with this simple, spacious turn- of the century townhouse.

The large and impressive armoire by the door
helps to convey the height of the room in which
it stands.

Bare polished floors harmonize with the clean lines of the rooms and a minimum of ornamental detail.

The entrance hall, with its massive front door and embroidered curtains, yields nothing to the present.

Like two works of art, the grand piano and the marble fireplace stand alone at the far end of the living room, reflected to infinity in the mirrored wall.

Tones of rose and
mauve are carried
out in this corner of
the living room.

Rampant Victorianism is given a full rein in the dining room.

Extensive remodeling has not destroyed the old-fashioned character of the kitchen.

This end of the living room by the fireplace has a comfortable, contemporary look.

Victorian furnishings reclaim the past in this unpretentious bedroom.

Urban Mansion-1889

Massive, rough-hewn stones give this Romanesque residence on the north side of the city a seriousness of purpose and a quality of permanence very different from the picturesque styles of the late 1800's. It was designed in 1889 by C. W. Palmer. In 1922, Ernest Graham, a partner in a prominent firm of architects, bought it and added on the section to the right of the mansion without disturbing the integrity of its style.

The exterior is a taffy-colored sandstone laid in a regular pattern on the ground floor and at random above. The doorway and the three windows over it have the typical Romanesque arch. One wing of the house has a domed roof while another section is topped with a conical roof. Projecting dormers with steep gables ring the entire attic floor. But these details are less important than the sheer weight of the house, with its richly textured stone surface.

The interior plan divides into four distinct sections. First is the rounded bay on the left of the facade, then the angled bay that includes the front entrance. The third bay, on the right, is also rounded, but with a flatter curve. Together, these three bays make up the house as Palmer designed it. Beginning with the trapezoid bay on the far right is the three-story section that Graham built.

Inside, the dimensions of the rooms imitate the stately proportions of the exterior. The entrance hall has tall fluted Corinthian columns embellished at the top with scrolls and acanthus leaves. Pilasters, a flattened version of the column, line the walls of the living room, dining room and entry. Their elaborate moldings, from the top of the capital to the cornice, complete this exercise in classic design.

Victorians treasured entrance halls as a sign of affluence and social prestige. More than passageways, their front halls announced the intentions of the rest of the house, occupying space just to show that space was abundant. They could be grand and pompous, yet beautiful, as is this one, which occupies the whole of one bay. In keeping with the passion for space, the living room, dining room and library each have their own bays. The service area and servants' quarters take up all three floors of Graham's addition. The third floor is reserved for playrooms and bedrooms for the children.

The Romanesque style had been reserved largely for use in public buildings until the architect H. H. Richardson adapted it so successfully to such private houses as the classic Glessner house on Chicago's south side. For city dwellers, the Romanesque style was a sensible choice. It provided a fortress with great solid walls to shut out the world and enclose a life of privacy and refinement.

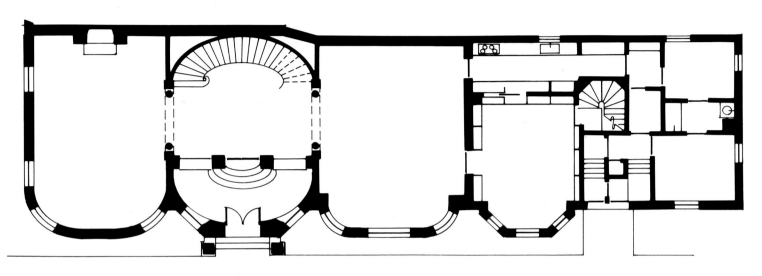

A seating arrangement at one end of the living room.

A daring convocation of decorative elements give the living room its unique, theatrical—and self-confident air.

Restored Romanesque-cir. 1889

This house, with the unmistakable strong, solid lines of the Richardson Romanesque style, similar to the one on page 57, was built about 1889. It is not a large house, but still it shares the emphatic rounded arch, the rough-hewn masonry and the sense of massiveness that typify Romanesque architecture.

Inside, this feeling has been reinforced by the unknown architect who used a light hand in carrying the medieval quality of the exterior through to the squared-off design of the bannister and wainscotting in the front hall. In contrast, the rest of the interior is richly picturesque.

The floor plan departs from the common arrangement of the period by shifting the dining room behind the stairs, allowing a place for a southern window that draws light into the main rooms of the house. This arrangement also allows the windows in the dining room—all much larger than is usual in a Romanesque house—to face into the small side yard and bring more light into the room.

Another appealing variation is the layout of the front bedroom. It includes a sitting room, with a fireplace and bay windows, and off the sitting room, an alcove for the bed. Small, high windows in the alcove provide light with privacy.

When the owners bought the house it was in a woeful state of decline, no room worse than the kitchen, with its rotting plaster, peeling linoleum and exposed plumbing. It is here that their remodeling work is most evident. Extensive replastering has been done throughout the house, the oak floors and paneling have been refurbished and the picture moldings have all been replaced.

Late eighteenth-century and nineteenth-century American furnishings add to the authentic flavor of the living room.

The upholstered chairs—handmade copies of an eighteenth-century style—are the only reproductions in the house.

Care and determination have been brought to the restoration of this house, as well as a single-minded devotion to the quality of its furnishings. But it does not have the atmosphere of a museum,

with invisible cords to keep you f◻ touching the treasure. In this hous◻ cious possessions are to be used◻ exist to add beauty to everyday li◻

The cherry four-poster in the master bedroom was made in 1810. The ornamental wooden screen that spans the entry from sitting room to bedroom was milled to the owner's specifications.

Woven baskets, cheery checked curtains, and copper cookware give a country look to this completely remodeled kitchen.

Towers and Turrets-1893

To describe a house as "Queen Anne" is to say simply that it was built toward the end of the nineteenth century. However, the label is used to describe a whole range of houses. During this late Victorian period, while much domestic architecture strove to recreate the symmetry and grandeur of certain periods—Classical and Colonial—other houses were going up that exuberantly and fearlessly combined elements from every style. Sometimes called "Picturesque Eclectic" as well as Queen Anne, they seemed cast in the image of the Vic-

torian parlor, all tassles and drapes and antimacassers. Some were pretty, others were grotesque. At its very best, the Queen Anne house was of free-flowing shape, emphasized the horizontal, and brought together a pleasant mix of design elements.

This house in a northern suburb of Chicago is an example of the style at its most controlled and elegant. Like the houses on page 86 and page 94, it was built in 1893.

Three strong horizontal bands over-
lay the totally asymmetrical pastiche
of spired turret, gables and bays, and
help pull the structure together. On
the first level there is the grand sweep
of the veranda, with its tall, narrow
windows descending almost to the
floor. On the second floor, an even row
of windows broader than the ones
below them comprises the second
band. The smaller windows on the third
floor, with their strong horizontal headings, make up the final band. Five
different paint colors delineate the
brackets and geometric designs that
break up the expanse of the clapboard
exterior.

The rooms on the main floor follow
the familiar pattern of living room,
parlor, dining room, with the kitchen
at the back. The wall dividing the living
room and parlor was removed in the
1930's, but even without that change,
the floor plan is one of unusual fluidity.

The house runs east and west so the public rooms to the right of the entry have a southern exposure. Because the house was built to one side of the property, all these rooms overlook a broad side yard. A double glass door connects the dining room to a sun porch, which opens onto the yard.

The slightly recessed front door on the north side of the house opens into a broad entryway. The vertical thrust of this gallerylike space is emphasized by the tall leaded glass windows set in a wood-paneled bay on the stairway's two-story wall.

On the second floor, the master bedroom at the front capitalizes on the semi-circular bay created by the turret. Pass-through closests—each with a built-in sink and a window—join the three bedrooms on this side of the house. These bedrooms can be closed off from the hallway to create a private

family suite. Across the hall is the guest
bedroom, with its own marble sink.

The third story consists entirely of
servants' quarters accessible only by
the back stairway—the usual Victorian
arrangement for employees who
shared the house but not the society
of their employers.

The Queen Anne and Picturesque
Eclectic styles are sometimes accused
of incoherence. But this house, as a
whole, is a fine example of the way
in which a variety of established
architectural forms can be assembled
inventively to create a pleasing design.

Even the master bath has its own small bay window, enlivened by a yellow stained glass center pane.

The rear of the house as seen from the garden echoes, in simplified form, the strong horizontal interest of the facade.

Northside Gothic-1893

This lively effusion of style and ornament is a Victorian Queen Anne house built in 1893 on Chicago's north side. The three-windowed bay at the front has a high steep roof adorned with a gothic gable. The corner turret with its conical roof is also frankly medieval. On the other hand, the restored wood porch has the decorative turned posts and filligreed pediment popularized by Eastlake in the late 1800's. This rash mixture of elements from different periods was common at the turn of the century.

The dark and intricate facade leaves the visitor unprepared for the bright clarity of the interior. The owners have chosen to modernize the interior of the house completely, and to redesign the back part of the second floor as a separate apartment.

A dramatic staircase, made with open treads of thick oak, zigzags up a broad skylighted shaft beginning at the left wall. This staircase dominates the house.

The small foyer has a red quarry tile floor and an oak plank ceiling. This warm, encircling combination is repeated in the kitchen and back hall. The living room and dining room run together along the right side of the house. They both retain their original wood-paneled bay window and fir plank floors. At the back of the first floor are a guest room, bath and two workrooms.

On the second floor, the master bedroom and sitting room have the feel of a loft suspended over the open stairs. An angled fireplace wall gives the rooms an unusual shape, but the original bay windows are still the focal points in each area.

There are those restorationists who believe that when an old house is put back together it should duplicate as closely as possible the intentions of the original architect, that the floor plan, materials and ornaments should be completely faithful to the original. This point of view has a lot of appeal—it argues for accuracy, for respect for the original designer and for the preservation of a historic artifact.

Past and present
meet at the foot of
the dramatic stair-
case. The original
wood-paneled
bay windows at
the front end of the
living room and
the fir plank floor
were refinished
by hand by the
owners.

What the owners have done here demonstrates a different, more practical approach to restoration. The exterior of the house remains undisturbed. The inside, of course, is completely changed. But not everything has been discarded. Much of the woodwork, the living room hearth and mantel and the decorative leaded glass in the windows are still intact. Preservation and practicality are kept in balance. The living spaces here are simple and attractive and the exterior still pays its respects to history.

Northside Revival-1893

T his house is in a neighborhood on the north side of the city that became a landmark district in the mid-1970's.

It was built in 1893 during an era of residential architecture called Classic and Colonial Revival, devoted to the imitation of historic styles, including those from America's own past. Architects studied these earlier styles and recreated them, sometimes precisely, for their clients. This Revivalist trend can be seen as a reaction to the excesses of many of the eclectic houses built since the Civil War —houses, like the one on page 86, that were often a catchall of unrelated and incompatible forms and patterns with no binding aesthetics.

Designed by the Chicago firm of Treat and Foltz, the house is based on an early American prototype, the Georgian house. The facade is balanced around an imposing central doorway framed by towering pilasters (similar to flattened columns). Two elements above the door are typically Georgian: the three-part arched Palladian window and the triangular pediment formed by the roof line. The raised basement, projecting eaves at the second and third floors, and the balustraded roof are also common features of this style.

When the current owners bought the building, the interior was in sad shape. They began the restoration by converting half the first floor into a separate rental apartment. The front door opens into a foyer that serves both the apartment and the remodeled main house. An elliptical staircase in the style of Adam leads from the entryway to the second floor where there are two living rooms, a dining room, kitchen and service area. Two interior walls have been removed on this floor to open up the space and to make more visible the pleasing, elongated form— somewhat like a paper clip—created by the circular bays at either end of the house. The ceilings on every floor have been lowered to accomodate heating and air conditioning ducts. This has meant sacrificing the decorative moldings on the walls, but the owners console themselves for this loss with the fact that most of these were already badly damaged and oddly mismatched.

The new interior has simple lines and includes some practical and modern variations on the original floor plan. The rounded rooms created by the bays are still the public rooms but now the kitchen, which is roomy enough for a breakfast table, adjoins one of the living rooms to create an area that suits family life, and also works for entertaining.

In accomplishing their remodeling, the owners have preserved the best of the past while still accommodating the needs of the present.

Southside Eclectic-1895

Here is another version of the eclectic Victorian architecture that goes under the name of Queen Anne. This one has a very solid, rather uncompromising look and its lines are boxier than the Queen Anne house on page 76, but the two share some general characteristics. Both rest on a raised stone-front basement and have the same pillared, wrap-around verandas. These encircling porches constitute the lowest of the three horizontal bands of emphasis that are typical of the Queen Anne style. In the house pictured here, the plain brick facing of the second floor makes up the middle band and the dark shingled roof the third and uppermost.

The house was built in 1895 on the south side of Chicago. The steep, complicated roof suggests towers and turrets and the irregularly shaped rooms that go with them, but the basic plan of the house is an only slightly irregular rectangle and the shape of the rooms is conventional. Among the fairly restrained mixture of Classical design details are the triangular pediment above the porch entrance, the ornate terracotta lintels over the windows and the paired Ionic columns supporting the porch roof.

The house appears to face the street but in fact the entrance is on the right side and all the rooms are oriented accordingly. The living room, to the left

of the entry, runs along the entire front of the house. The butternut-paneled dining room fits into the bay just to the right of the entry. Behind it is a small study within a shallow bay. A door in the dining room leads into a butler's pantry which connects with the kitchen. The second floor is given over to bedrooms (three of them with fireplaces) and to three large baths. The top story has a studio and two more bedrooms. These are only accessible by a back staircase, as the third floor was originally intended for servants' quarters.

The massive but simple overall shape of this house puts its narrow city lot to maximum use. The walls reach nearly to the property lines, leaving the porch to serve as the outdoor area. Consequently, the floor plan allows for lots of large rooms—an effect as appealing now as it was at the turn of the century.

The fireplace in the dining room has two unusual features: a window above the mantel (which requires a double flue) and carved columns with the sinuous lines of Art Nouveau. The centerpiece on the dining table is a rare eighteenth-century Leeds creamware cocklepot.

An assembly of rare collectibles is displayed on a handsome marble table. At the far left, is an example of the elaborate decorative pottery of Obadiah Sherratt, an early nineteenth-century English ceramicist.

A lady in evening dress presides over this exquisite still-life in old glass.

Grande Dame-1899

Among the many buildings that constitute the rich architectual personality of Chicago are several old grande dames in the Loop and along the Lake Shore, all designed by one architect whose name is practically unknown.

Benjamin Marshall had no formal education in architecture, yet in 1895, at the age of 21, he was a full partner in the firm of Wilson and Marshall. His career began with large commissions and lasted for many years.

Marshall was at home with a variety of Revival styles whose pretentions he eventually managed to tame. He designed the fabulous Iroquois Theater in 1903, which was later gutted by a devastating fire. Still standing are the Blackstone Hotel, the apartments at the curve of East Lake Shore Drive and the distinctive South Shore Country Club.

This imposing house on the south side of the city was designed and built by Marshall in 1899. It is a good example of Italianate Revival style.

The house takes the form of a single rectangular mass. Deep bracketed eaves, quoins (corner inserts originally used to reinforce stonework) and string courses (horizontal applied decoration) enrich the formal balance of the facade. The most ornate elements on the exterior are the small balconies supported by heavily carved brackets and the elaborate ironwork balustrades.

Marshall designed the main floor for formal entertaining, then provided two more rooms for family living. A little door under the stairs allows access to the basement and the "log cabin" room, with its rough-hewn log paneling and a stone fireplace, which might be considered the Victorian equivalent of the modern "rumpus room."

The impressive central staircase rises all the way to the third floor, lit by a stained glass skylight set in a vaulted ceiling and visible from the ground floor.

Marshall's arrangment of rooms on the second floor is one that he was to use frequently in the luxury apartments he designed later in his career. Each bedroom is connected to a bath and a dressing room with elaborate built-in shelves and cupboards. A sitting room adjoins the master bedroom.

The master bathroom illustrates perfectly Marshall's gift for working with ornamental, as well as practical, detail. The walls and fixtures are all marble. A handpainted plaster frieze of rolicking cherubs runs along the top of the walls. Above the tub there is a small window laminated with a hand-screened fabric in a floral design. The tub itself is the centerpiece of the bathroom. A shower head suspended over the middle is easily the size of a dinner plate. The pipe arching over it descends into a structure that resembles a silver samovar. This is a holding tank with hot and cold controls; a thermometer allows the bather to adjust the water temperature before stepping under the shower. A gas fire in the bathroom wall insures the comfort of the bather on chilly days. Beneath the tile floors, a drainage system runs through lead troughs that catch the condensation from the pipes. Amazingly, all these devices still work.

On the third floor are the usual ser-vants' rooms at the rear, and a ballroom at the front. The ballroom was a turn-of-the-century extravagance that many large Victorian homes enjoyed. This one has a Moorish motif and a high-recessed ceiling sprinkled with tiny lights to simulate stars. A dressing room near the ballroom is designated as the "fainting room" on the original floor plans. The image this phrase evokes—of pampered ladies, gowned and gloved, laced into complicated corsets—exactly suits the tone of this extraordinary turn-of-the-century house.

This charming room, perhaps originally intended as a library, is hidden away behind the staircase in the hall and connects with the living room.

The general feeling of richness and elegance throughout the house is reasserted in the elaborately carved rosewood paneling in the dining room.

This corner grate, with its fleur de lys tiles, is one more example of the architect's attention to detail.

A hand-painted plaster frieze of rolicking cherubs runs along the top of the walls in the master bathroom. A gas fire insures the comfort of the bather on chilly days.

This structure, which resembles a silver samovar, is actually a holding tank with hot and cold controls; a thermometer allows the bather to adjust the water temperature before stepping under the shower.

An old-fashioned footbath makes an interesting cache-pot for a flourishing begonia.

Renovated Storefront
cir. 1900

Most people would be surprised to discover that this commonplace storefront building on Chicago's north side is a single family dwelling. The building dates from the turn of the century and originally it housed a bakery.

Just inside the centered doorway is a gray-carpeted foyer. A short flight of stairs at the right of the entry leads to a landing and from here the drama of the house is visible.

At the center of the house is an atrium, two stories high, that occupies fully a third of the length of the house. A gallery runs along the left wall slightly above the level of the landing. This level connects the rooms on the second floor, back to front. A low wall separates the gallery from a broad ledge that is actually the roof of the first-floor study. An indoor garden on top of the ledge gets sunshine from the skylights directly above it.

From the landing, another flight of stairs leads down to the gallery at the right of the first-floor level.

The wide open area of the atrium eliminates the usual horizontal lines of distinction between one floor and another. The living room is at the back of the first level overlooking the garden, while the kitchen and dining area take up the back of the second. The bedrooms stack up vertically at the front of the house.

A study lined with books is enclosed by a curved wall that separates it from the living room. Tucked away at the front of the ground floor is the nursery.

Running the whole width of the building at the second-floor level is the master bedroom. Here, a bay window forms an alcove that is used as a sitting room.

Behind the unimposing face of this simple, gray limestone facade is a home with all the luxuries of light and space that are so hard to come by in the middle of the city.

Prairie House-1901

While most architects at the turn of the century were working within the conventions of historical styles, Frank Lloyd Wright was already designing houses that were the progenitors of all modern residential architecture. He did not jettison overnight every traditional element of design, but he did distill the past into something wholly new.

This house, built by Wright in 1901 (just two years after the Grande Dame residence on page 106 was finished), is one of the first that he called his "prairie houses." Its dimensions are

modest and its building costs were low by turn-of-the-century standards. In fact, soon after it was built, *House Beautiful* featured it as a home for people whose first requirement was economy.

While not as earth-hugging as some of its successors, this house still meets the ground decisively, without the paraphernalia of raised basements or verandas so common at the time. The intersecting gables of the roof have the broad, overhanging eaves that were to become a Wright signature. Bands of casement windows, repeated in various dimensions, around the corners of the house are also typical. The geometric patterns in the leaded glass have a prismatic effect that causes the windows to seem opaque from the outside. Wright himself designed the patterns, creating new ones for each of his prairie houses.

The plan followed here can be seen as a modified cross, with the main

rooms radiating out from the center. No doors divide the rooms on the first floor, but the overall shape of the house distinctly separates one space from another.

The only deviation from the original floor plan is in the kitchen, where a pantry wall has been removed to enlarge the space. The only alteration to the outside of the house has been the addition of a deck off the kitchen.

Upstairs, only a low interior wall separates the study from the stairwell. The windows running along two sides of this balcony-like area draw light down into the center of the house.

Wright had a great preference for natural materials and a liking for earthy colors. Here, the owners have remained true to Wright's taste. The wall coverings, many of them grass cloth, are in warm tones of gold, beige and orange. All the woodwork has been stripped to reveal the original dark gumwood that stands out in high relief against the lighter walls and gives the interior its Japanese feeling. In furnishing the house, the owners have been able to track down a few original Wright pieces.

In spite of certain hallmarks of material and design, there is no one consistent look to a Wright house. Each one is different. Brick, concrete, wood and stucco are used in various combinations. Innovative details of design are variously applied. Wright's enormous influence as an architect stems not so much from the particulars of the prairie house as from his sense of place and his feeling for natural materials. He found new ways to structure space, replacing boxes with the low, rambling, open-plan buildings that were the first truly American architecture.

The brick fireplace at one end of the living room stands within a niche created by a lowered ceiling and built-in benches on either side. The globe-shaped andirons were designed by Wright.

The crisp lines of the book shelves and wood trim continue from the living room into the dining room.

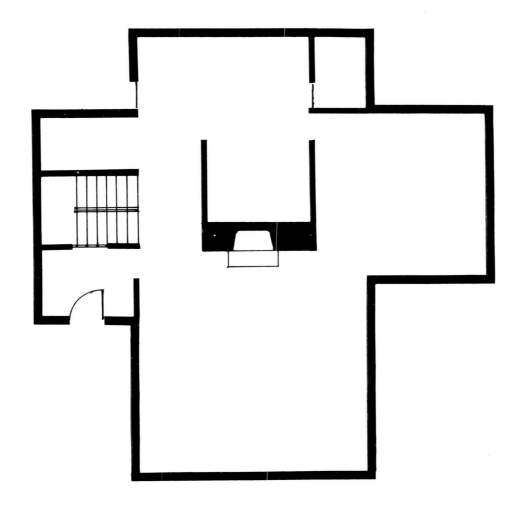

The desk and lamp in the master bedroom
are both of Wright's design.

Grass cloth on the walls of the master
bedroom follows the preference of the
architect for natural materials.

Colonial Revival-1903

T his rather ungainly house in Chicago's south side was built in 1903. The design, a mixture of Early American styles, belongs to Colonial Revival. The two heavy dormers with their swan's neck pediments, the high rounded window headings on the first floor, along with the distinct quoins at the corner are typical of the Revival style. However seemingly incompatible its various elements of design, the house overrides them nicely with its unmistakable sense of itself.

Inside, the layout of the rooms is

simple and functional. The living room occupies most of the front, to the right of the entrance hall. Behind it is the library, enclosed by a large bay window. The dining room is further to the rear, leading into a recessed service area and kitchen. On the left, between the kitchen and the entrance hall, is a small sitting room. The second floor has four bedrooms and a study. The third floor is one large open space which lends itself well to use as a game room.

However, in this particular house the rooms are not so much spaces for living as they are a showcase designed to set off the owners' large and remarkable

collection of art. Every wall and surface in every room is covered with graphics, paintings and objects. The living room, crammed with pieces of folk art and other more bizarre artifacts, looks much more like an extravagant set for *Babes In Toyland* than a Victorian parlor.

Upstairs, fans, beaded evening bags, old perfume bottles, dolls, masks and snow scenes under glass are all to be found in various places. Only in the bathroom, with its leaded casement window, does utility enjoy pre-eminence.

The owners' willingness to share so much space with their collection reflects their strong sensibility to art. The collective effect of their house is joyous, sometimes funny, often tactile and always completely personal.

In the entrance hall, a life-size Segal figure rests on a bench in a mood of cool, white patience.

It is a surprise to discover that the red velvet chair in a corner of the living room, adorned with curving steer horns, is not a piece of soft sculpture, but an antique from the American West.

Prairie Idiom-1908

Built in 1908 on the north side of the city, this familiar looking house demonstrates as clearly as any how quickly the conventions of the Prairie School architecture were taken up by other architects and builders and translated into everyday American homes.

The house pictured here is not in the pure Prairie style. It is a cross breed clearly influenced by Wright and his disciples. Taken from the Prairie style are the low-pitched roof with broad overhanging eaves, the strong horizontal elements of the wide porch, the bands of windows on the second and third floors and the concrete sill at the base of the house. More superficial associations with the style are the stucco exterior with dark wood trim, and the concrete flower urns on either side of the porch steps, often seen in Wright's own designs. But the floor plan is decidedly Victorian.

The entryway has three areas. First, there is a vestibule with an inner door. Next, a narrow hall runs between a library on the left and the living room on the right. This hall finally broadens to meet the stairway at the center of the left wall. Straight ahead are the pantry and kitchen. To the right, behind the living room, is the impressive dining room. This is the only room that lies across the front-to-back axis of the house. It bows out into a bay window—the only element that modifies the plan's perfect rectangle. While most of the rooms have quiet lines and simple moldings, the dining room is decked out with rich oak wainscotting and ceiling trim.

Color and contrast work
together to make this
an unusually attractive
entrance hall.

Beyond the dining room are a butler's pantry and a sunny, enclosed porch, now used as a breakfast room.

On the second floor the rooms form a U-shape around the spacious central stair hall. The master bedroom is large and airy. It catches the morning sun through its oversized bay window. A dressing room links the bedroom to a study. All the rooms on the right side of this floor have connecting doors, in addition to the doors that lead to the central hall. Finally, a nursery occupies the back left corner of the second floor.

The third floor is cut up by eaves but is still large enough to hold a work room and a guest room.

Like most hybrids, this cross between the Prairie style and Victorian traditions has produced a vigorous strain. Two and three-story houses with the same broad porch, central dormer and simple geometric structure became the suburban style house, built from 1910 to 1930, that is so common to Chicago's neighborhoods and indeed to most small towns in America.

The exuberance of the painting over the couch beckons the eye to this side of the living room.

Books, rugs and
comfortably up-
holstered furniture
bring a rich livabil-
ity to this area of
the room.

The large and airy master bedroom, with its over-sized bay window which catches the early morning sun, is refreshingly lacking in a "decorator look."

The glass front bookcases at one end of the living room were brought back by the owners from the Philippines.

The tones and textures of various woods soften the lines of a modern kitchen.

Chicago Tudor-1911

The early 1900's introduced no great change in the architectural taste of the upper and middle classes in Chicago. At the beginning of this new century, what most well-to-do people wanted was a setting from the past: the Colonial houses of their forefathers, a Tudor manor or a French provincial farmhouse.

This house in a northern suburb of the city was designed by Ernest Mayo in 1911. It has many stylistic elements that follow quite literally its archetype, the Elizabethan manor. The half-timbering and the high-peaked gables edged with vergeboard, the complicated roofline, the slight overhang of the upper stories and the small-paned, leaded glass windows are all faithfully Elizabethan.

The interior shares many ingredients with its English model. Heavy, bracketed beams of dark wood and a huge stone fireplace in the living room suggest a medieval hunting hall. The plaster walls in the front hall are carefully etched to resemble massive stone blocks. In contrast to the living room, the dining room, originally designed as a music room, has an airy and feminine look because of the moldings, the bay windows and the lavishly ornate mantel.

Beyond the living room are two more

common rooms divided by an almost full wall of leaded glass. The room on the far side of the windowed wall boasts French doors flanking an elaborate marble fountain. It doubles in brass as both a veranda and a second living room.

On the second floor, the master bedroom opens into a large sitting room with a southern exposure. At the rear, servants' quarters extend over the kitchen wing to create a nearly self-contained service area. More rooms for servants over the garage clearly indicate that cooks, maids and chauffeurs were a vital part of upper-middle-class life before World War I.

Although the kind of life this house represents did not survive the Great War, its architecture did as reverence for the graceful symbols of past cultures kept pace with modernism far into the twentieth century.

Oak floors, pan-
eled wainscotting
and beamed ceil-
ings give a decid-
edly Tudor feeling
to these adjoining
living areas.

*The spacious brick
terrace is big
enough for large
scale entertaining.*

Converted Garage

1922

This attractive townhouse was once a commercial garage. It was built in 1922 on the fringe of a neighborhood, now a landmark district, which has the charm that derives from low buildings and narrow, tree-lined streets.

When the current owners bought the building, a gas pump still stood in the center of the main floor. But in addition to the pump there was a side yard that could be converted to a garden—a rare find in the center of the city.

The facade of the house is completely undistinguished. It is on the inside that the house comes into its own. One long wall divides the first floor into two spaces. On one side of the wall a hall, with storage and service areas, leads to the back of the house. On the other side is a vast rectangular space interrupted

upholstered chairs and sofas, one under a skylight and one in front of the fireplace, bring the dramatic proportions of the living room down to a manageable scale.

Behind the fireplace wall, a low buffet at right angles to the wall of bookshelves suggests a separation between the dining area and kitchen. But no attempt has been made to conceal the main work area of the kitchen, red-tiled and hung with copper pots, which projects part way into the dining area.

In the far corner of the room, opposite the bookshelf wall, floor-to-ceiling windows form two sides of yet another area. The oak flooring ends to

form a graveled square on which rests an antique drawing table, framed by an array of lush green plants.

only briefly by a short central fireplace wall with openings at either side. Floor-to-ceiling French doors open into the garden that runs the length of the building. Opposite these doors is a dramatic, 40-foot stretch of book-shelves that adds much to the character of the room.

Two clusters of comfortably

A collection of toys and stuffed animals tell whom this room belongs to.

Two clusters of upholstered chairs and sofas, one under the skylight and one in front of the fireplace, bring the dramatic proportions of the living room down to manageable size.

Gleaming wooden tables, fresh flowers and family mementos give a nice sense of intimacy to the living room.

Upstairs there are three bedrooms, two baths and a cedar deck extending out from the master suite.

The harmony and interest of this house seem particularly remarkable when you remember that all this richness and contour has been superimposed on the simplest of geometric forms, in a building as bare and unenticing as a shoebox.

Ex-urban Chateau-1932

I t is hard to believe that this house, built on a rise in the midst of wooded countryside remote from Chicago's smoky urban heart, is still only 30 minutes from the Loop by train.

It was built in 1932 to the specifications of the original owner, who had wanted to duplicate, turret for turret, a chateau he had seen in Burgundy. Fortunately, he chose to do this at a time when there were architects available who were still willing to take

on such a job. Within a few years, by 1940, the vogue for Revival architecture would be over.

In spite of its overall loyalty to the architecture of the French countryside, there is an amusing element of dualism in this house which reproduces a chateau on one facade (facing the garden) and a French-Norman farmhouse on the other (facing the drive). But its self-conscious quaintness works. The house looks quite genuine, sitting easily at the top of a rise against a background of

oaks, pines and maples. The well-trimmed tiers of the formal garden extending down the slope to the pool could easily be mistaken for a scene in Burgundy.

The exterior is a mixture of brick, stucco and board, all painted white, beneath a steep, shingled roof. Tall, multi-paned windows and evenly spaced dormers give character to the chateau side. The octagonal turret to the left of the house as it faces the garden is typically French Provincial. The farmhouse side is more irregular. It has odd angles, large chimneys and a central, shorter turret.

The main entrance is through this smaller turret that creates a foyer in the shape of a perfect circle. A short hall runs behind the foyer, connecting the kitchen to the right, the living room to the front and the stairs to the bedrooms to the left.

At the far right end of the kitchen is another hallway leading to the pine-paneled dining room. A greenhouse, added by the current owners, is joined to this passageway.

The dining room takes its shape from the large turret. Here, the durability of Irish linen is undeniable: the earth-tone drapes are the same ones that were hung in 1932.

From the dining room a hall and a short flight of steps lead down to the sunken living room. Bookshelves line the living room walls, interrupted only by an eighteenth century French marble fireplace on one side and French doors overlooking the garden on the other.

A complicated series of stairs off the living room lead to the master bedroom and to another bedroom over the garage. Also off these stairs is a guest bedroom on the main floor. This is an entirely new room built in the space between the garage and the main wing, with doors opening onto a terrace garden.

The master bedroom occupies the entire main wing above the living room. The steep pitch of the roof creates an angled wall that is punctuated with deepset dormer windows.

The overall floor plan is sprawling and even haphazard. Nevertheless, the architect has arranged it so that each of the main rooms faces the panoramic view of the surrounding country. While today it may not be the most practical house to live in, it still boasts the mellowness and charm of the originals on which it was based.

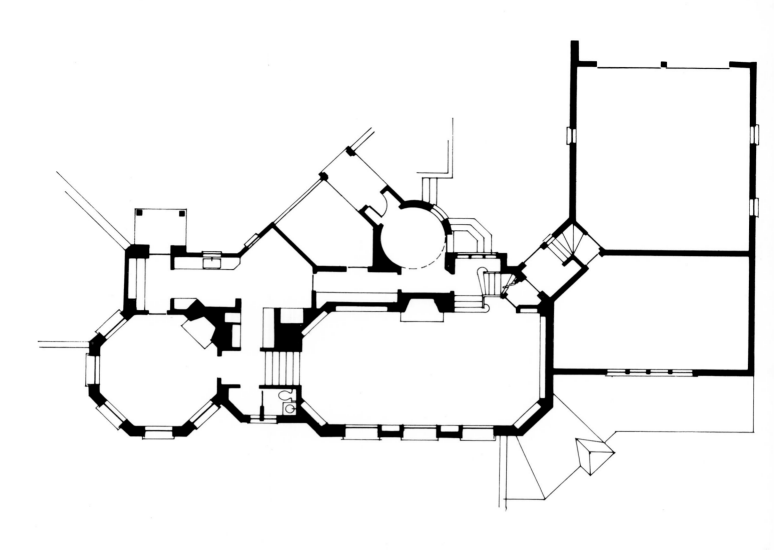

Handsome built-in black walnut cabinets, in keeping with the provincial spirit of the rest of the house, line one wall of a newly added guestroom. French doors open onto a terrace garden.

Bookshelves line the sunken living room,
interrupted only by an eighteenth-century
French marble fireplace on one side and
French doors, overlooking the garden, on
the other.

Georgian Manor-1934

David Adler was an architect for the very rich. From 1912 to 1935 he produced plans for dozens of houses, largely for Chicago socialites. Most of them were vast "country" homes in the city's far northern suburbs, designed to look like the Villa d'Este, a chateau in the Dordogne, or a Spanish hacienda.

Adler's interest in his houses was not confined to the drawing board. He oversaw every detail of landscaping, interior design and even the furnish-

ings. On frequent trips to Europe he would buy mantels, floors, paneling, furniture, and sometimes even whole rooms. His houses resembled sumptuous stage sets whose size and magnificence were worthy of the incomes of their owners.

This house, with its symmetrical Early American look, was completed in 1934 (in the midst of the Depression). The central doorway with an arched heading, the 12-paned window, twin chimneys and dormers are character-

istically Georgian. Two side walls extend at right angles from either end of the house to form a courtyard. Each wall ends in a small building resembling an outpost at the gate. Whitewashed red brick gives the house a warm, pink glow.

The plan of the house can be understood as four bays radiating out from a slightly irregular rectangle. The bays are each two stories high, while the central body of the house is three stories.

Beyond the entry, which is set forward from the main rooms, a gallery of baronial proportions connects the various bays. To the right of the foyer, at the southern end of the house, is the living room bay. It is a very long room with restrained moldings and wainscotting in the Federal style.

The two bays of the library and the dining room are perpendicular to the gallery and project fairly far from the back of the central rectangle. The paneling in the library was taken from a seventeenth-century English country house.

Between the library and dining room there is a long sunroom with a marble floor and elaborate Chippendale pilasters set at intervals along the wall.

167

In the dining room the intricate mantel is the work of Charles II's court carver. Because Adler fitted existing paneling into new rooms, he often had to create jogs and niches to accommodate the importations. Here, he built two china cabinets to fit the dimensions of the English woodwork.

To the left of the house the final bay is given to the kitchen and service area.

The second floor has five bedrooms as well as servants' quarters in the rear. The master suite includes a dressing room, a bathroom with goldplated fixtures, a bedroom with a Chippendale fireplace and a sitting room in the

sunny south bay. Three other bedrooms on this floor have antique wood paneling imported from Europe, while a fourth has antique wallpaper hand-painted in a bamboo and pheasant design. When Adler found that he did not have enough of the original

paper to cover the room, he simply
commissioned an artist to copy the
design.

On the third floor are more
bedrooms and a small separate
apartment.

In designing the outside of this house,
Adler has followed the rules of a classic
American architectural style. Inside,
he has set the stage with an amazing
pastiche of European cultures, using
authentic artifacts from the past to do
so. It might be said that in designing
this impressive residence he did not so
much build a house as create an
alternate world.

Twin columns suggest the proscenium of a richly furnished stage set in this view from the foyer to the gallery, which connects the various bays of the house.

*Seventeenth-century paneling, taken from
an English country house, enrich the walls of
the library.*

Gold-plated fixtures, an oriental rug and parquet flooring make this master bathroom one of the most beautiful and luxurious in the world.

Ornamental details like these add to the feeling of elegance in Adler's houses.

Antique French wall paneling frames
eleventh-century Southeast Asian canvas-
on-wood paintings in a room that was
designated on the original floor plan as a
"dressing room" for women guests.

The elaborate molding over the Chippendale fireplace makes an enchanting perch for a collection of ceramic birds.

Paneling imported from Europe and a pair
of rare antique beds give a quiet beauty to
this guest bedroom.

The Engineered House-1951

By the 1930's, houses began to have the look of what we recognize today as modern architecture, with its assembly of steel grids, reinforced concrete and glass walls. Turning their backs on the past, more and more architects began to see in products of the machine age the possibility for a new aesthetic—linear, direct and, above all, functional.

The Chicago architect George Fred Keck approached the house as a problem in engineering rather than an exercise in style. He believed that every feature of a house, from its glass walls to its louvres, had a purpose.

Radiant heating in the concrete slab and in the ceiling supplements the natural source of heat from the sun. Narrow panels, consisting of adjustable louvres, are spaced along the glass walls. Inside, solid wood shutters conceal and insulate the louvres in winter; in warm weather they pull open to catch the breeze.

Keck and his brother, William, designed this house for a site in a northern suburb of the city in 1951. It sits on a cliff above the Lake Michigan shore, buffered from the highway by acres of wooded land. The side facing a private road is a uniform, almost blank sand-colored brick, interrupted only by a glass, box-like entry with a flat canopy roof.

Most of the rooms line up single file along a gradual arc that forms the main wing. The eastward side of the house, facing the lake, is walled with tall sheets of glass that continue around to make up the southern wall as well. The tress and water become part of the landscape of the rooms.

The Kecks were pioneers in passive solar energy. From the 1930's on, they built houses with large expanses of window oriented to the sun, aware that this alone could save 15 to 20 percent in heating costs. Here, this natural source of heat supplements radiant heating in the concrete slab and in the ceilings. Broad eaves over the southern walls control excessive summer heat.

There are four parts to the house, with clear-cut boundaries between them. The entryway is the center. Its black slate floor begins outside the front door, encompasses the dining room to the left and extends beyond it outside, where it forms a patio. This section and the six-room service area beyond are one story high. The dining room wall extends beyond the house and marks the end of the patio. It also serves to cut off the kitchen and servants' quarters from the rest of the house.

To the right of the front door an oak parquet floor coincides with the beginning of the two-story section of the house and continues through it. This contains the study and the living room downstairs, and two bedrooms above.

The living room is pure line and scale, drawing the eye to the monolithic fireplace, a marble shaft inside a glass tower filled with plants.

The master bedroom, with a parquet floor, shares the fireplace wall on the second floor and overhangs the garden. A door in a small alcove off this room opens onto an outside stairway that descends along the garden tower. A dressing room adjoins the bedroom. Here, and in the guest room next door, the parquet floor continues, adding

interest to the deliberate bareness of the house.

The third section of the house is a one-story wing that stretches away from the lake side rooms. It is connected to the main house by a short, glass-lined hall that also has doors leading to the grounds and to the driveway. This wing contains a den and two children's rooms. The fourth section is a matching wing at the opposite end of the house, comprised of a garage and service rooms.

This house was built only seventeen years after the house designed for wealthy clients, but the resemblance ends there. In a short space of time, the beauty of simplicity gained an equal footing with opulence.

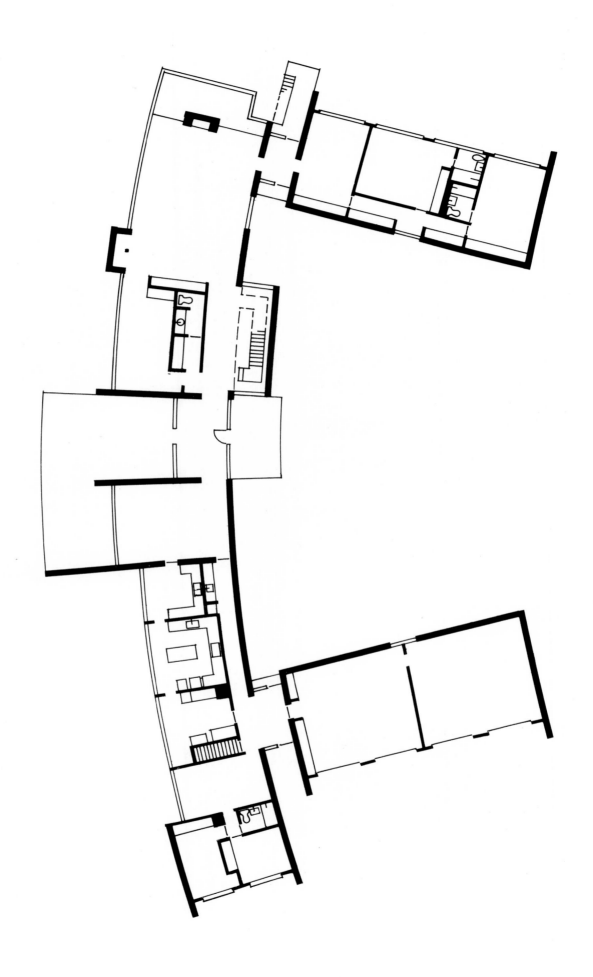

The Wright Tradition-1967

Edward Dart was a Chicago architect who brought the traditions of the Prairie School into contemporary architecture. His feeling for natural materials and his mastery of the open plan, both elements associated with Wright, are most evident in this house, built in 1967, that stands on a hillside in the northwest suburb of the city.

The central core of the building begins slightly below ground with the front entrance and rises three-and-a-half stories. Its two wings spread out over the slopes of the hill. The exterior of the house is a combination of brick and wood shingles.

The front door, entered from a porch, is at the lowest level. At the end of the porch, two square brick columns support a band of etched concrete. This temple form design is the first of several acknowledgements to Wright. The front door itself has a geometric pattern of wood strips, suggesting Wright's leaded glass windows. To the left of the entryway, stretching down the hill, there is a guest room, a study and two garages.

Free-standing stairs lead from the front door up into the lofty spaces of the central core of the house. The rooms on the main floor radiate from the staircase and encircle it. The exaggerated height of the vaulted ceiling would perhaps be overpowering except for the devices Dart has used to moderate its effect, among them a network of heavy wood beams which extends into the upper regions of the house. These rising beams and the suspended platforms they support break up the towering space and bring it down to a less imposing scale. Spanning the rooms about eight feet above the floor, horizontal beams not only imply a low ceiling but mark off specific areas within the rooms.

The principal rooms run along the south wall. Sliding glass doors with deep overhanging eaves overlook a small lake at the bottom of the rise.

Over the fireplace in the living room, Dart has designed a concrete mantel that repeats the design of the cornice on the front porch. In one corner of this room there is a sitting area defined by its sunken glazed brick floor. Beyond this is the dining room which adjoins the kitchen.

The master bedroom, with a bath

and dressing room, is behind the fireplace wall. Sliding glass doors lead to a terrace shared by the living room.

Two more bedrooms and a study occupy the opposite end of the house.

High above the main rooms are two platforms that Dart called the "crow's nests." The surrounding windows look out over the rolling hills on all sides.

Dart's easiness with space, his feeling of connection with the land and his choice of materials are all part of the Prairie School heritage.

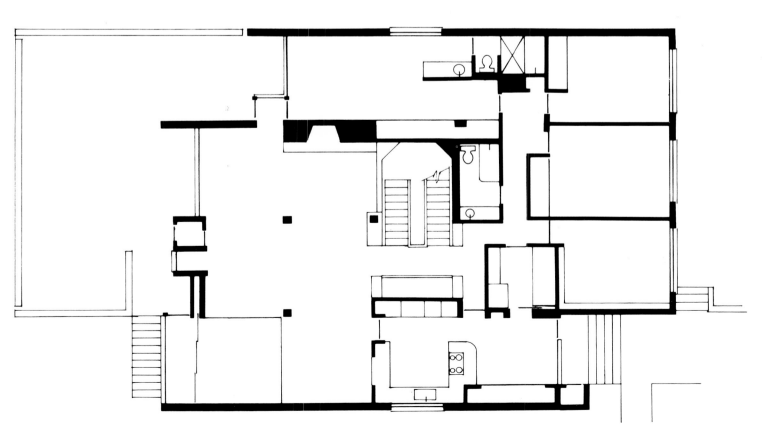

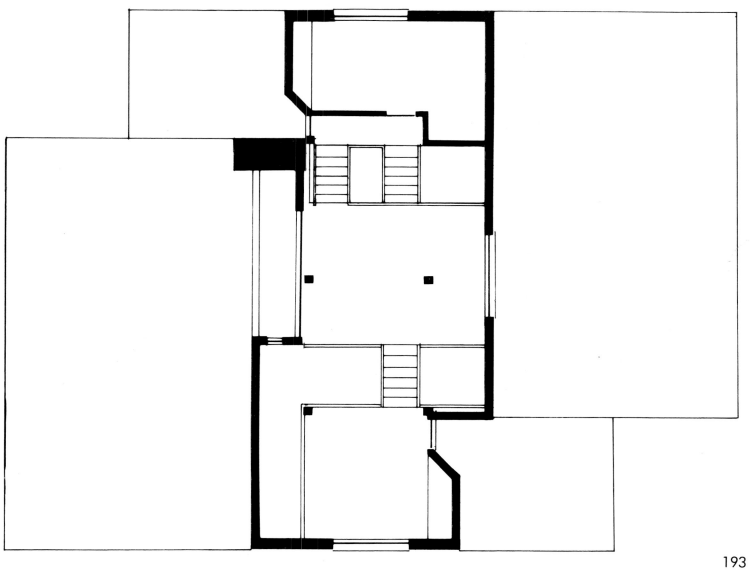

Animal Crackers-1978

T his boisterous cedar and stucco house, completed in 1978, sits on a wooded corner lot in a northern suburb of the city.

The architect, Stanley Tigerman, calls it "Animal Crackers." When the first scale model of the house was painted red, blue and yellow and set down next to the familiar cookie box, the resemblance was clear.

The house is not isolated, but its neighbors are at some distance because of the large size of the lots in the area. What might have seemed outrageous in a starchy row of conventional houses here seems casual, intimate and imaginative.

In addition to its waggish silhouette, the exterior has a number of design flourishes. There are large windows shaped like grand piano tops and small

rectangular windows that line the walls from top to bottom. In a final spirit of whimsy, the architect has used exposed gutters and downspouts to frame the windows on two sides of the house.

The general plan is very uncomplicated. The garage is a single-story cube appended to the main house, a two-story cube. The two-story living area has a den, living room, enclosed porch, dining room, kitchen and laundry at the ground level. All of these rooms are contained within the perimeter of a simple square except for the kitchen, which extends out along the side of the garage. The second floor has a master bedroom with attached dressing room and bath; a second bedroom and bath; and a study.

If the windows seem playful on the outside, inside they have a completely different effect. Rooms that might otherwise seem unrelentingly square and plain take on an airyness and serenity with their exposure to nearby trees.

However out of the ordinary the outside of the house, the interiors are very subdued. The one departure from the understated tone of the decor is the long blue wall in the living room. A work of art in the form of a neon cloud mounted there appears to float across this make-believe sky.

Together, the architect and his clients have built a practical and economical house with enough sense of fun to deserve its name.

Sculpted Space-1980

This quiet, understated house was designed by the Chicago architect Laurence Booth. Completed in 1980, it stands on a one-acre lot in a subdivision of a northern suburb of the city where there is still undeveloped land. A fairly thick strip of woods runs along the back and around one side of the site.

To appreciate it fully, the intentions of the designer must be explained. Booth believes that contemporary architects, in their concern for technology, have often lost sight of human experience. A house, he will tell you, is first of all a place for people to live—not just a monotonous exercise in structural engineering. Here, he wanted to build a house of open, continuous space, without the sharp angles that often confine human movement.

From the outside, the house gives the appearance of a flat, unarticulated rectangle, long and low. The exterior surface is a medium-brown stucco, with no windows visible from the street. However, the effect is not stark. It is rather of something crafted and compact, set down gently among the softer textures of the surrounding trees.

If the outside of the house seems two-dimensional, the interior meets the eye with a series of gentle arcs and angles that open out into unexpected volumes of sculptured space.

Basically, the house is made up of one large rectangle with a much smaller rectangle at one end, forming an el. The main rooms—a family room, dining room, livingroom and study—align along an arbitrary angle that runs diagonally through the larger rectangle. These rooms, each with its own arced ceiling, are open to a long, skylighted gallery. The rooms are well defined but not quite separate: they all draw space and light from the gallery. The diagonal line ends at the master bedroom and bath that take up one end of the large rectangle.

The smaller rectangle is primarily given over to two bedrooms for the owners' teenage boys. Also, at this end of the house, a family room, kitchen and breakfast room work together to form one functional unit.

Throughout the house, various design elements convey a sense of softness and serenity. The arc of the ceilings is repeated in various ways in each room. Built-in shelves in the study and master bedroom also echo the curve.

Certain pieces of furniture, designed by the architect, repeat the curving lines and round edges which are one of the outstanding features of this low-keyed house which, however subdued, exerts a soft power.

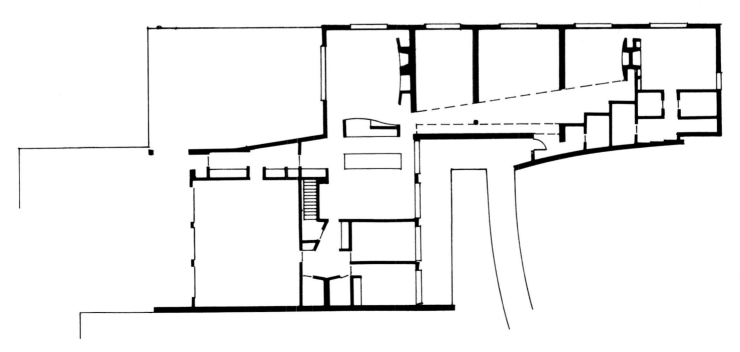

Glass House-1980

However up-to-date it may still look, the transparent house made its appearance in the U.S. in the late 1920's. Imported from Europe, the International style looked to machine-made materials, such as steel and concrete, and put them to use in a way that emphasized the function of the house rather than any romantic or historical traditions of architecture.

This cool and unconfiding house, designed by the firm of Krueck and Olsen, was built in 1980 on the north side of the city. The front presents a lattice-work of highly defined rectangles of varying size and opacity. The facade divides itself into distinct sections that correspond to the interior plan of the house.

On the left, vertical rectangles frame the two-story exterior vestibule. Just visible through fine steel grating is a dramatic curved glass brick interior wall that encloses a circular staircase.

To the right of the vestibule section, marked off on the facde, is a narrow ladder of glass panes defining the area of the foyer. This transparent strip continues up to the roof, traversing its entire length and coming to a stop at the base of the rear wall. Inside, the long, narrow slice of space defined by this strip of glass serves as a hallway connecting all the parts of the house.

At ground level, the facade.to the right of the foyer has three solid squares. The first conceals an interior hallway, the others cover the garage. Above these squares is a regular pattern of semi-opaque panes that form one wall of the second-floor master suite. The walls of the house that overlook neighboring property are sheathed with ribbed metal siding.

Three interlocking rectangles make up the geometric C-shape of the house that encloses three sides of an outdoor courtyard. The two-story living room space is centered on the long side of the C and matches the width of the courtyard. Its polished terrazzo floor extends throughout the first floor. A glass block bridge on the inside wall connects the front and back wings. This walkway is suspended directly beneath the long skylight. At the far end of the living room, there is a dining area defined by a lowered ceiling, a free-standing storage unit and a glassed-in garden. Sliding glass walls separate the dining area from the kitchen at the back.

Opaque glass doors on one side of the kitchen open into the pantry and laundry room. Another door leads to the servant's room.

On the second floor above the dining room area is a library overlooking the living room. A partial wall holds a simple, elevated marble fireplace and shelving. A guest room and sundeck occupy the rest of the back wing on this level.

The master bedroom in the front wing includes a free-standing bathroom. White ceramic tiles face the outside walls of the bath, as well as every inside surface—walls, ceilings, cabinets and floors.

Furnishings have been kept to a minimum. Personal possessions are stored away in an integrated storage system that is part of the architecture of the interior. The detached and noncommittal character of the house represents the pursuit of a single idea: the subordination of style to function.

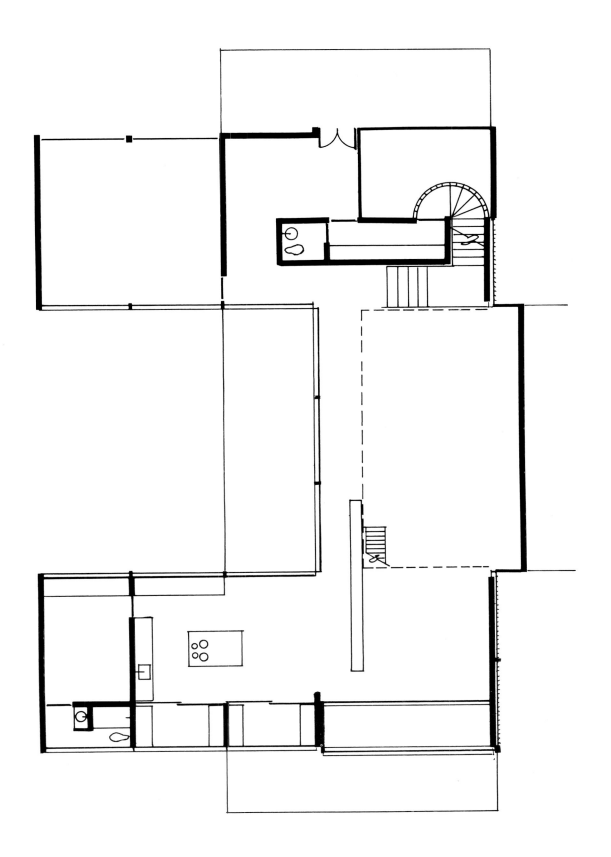

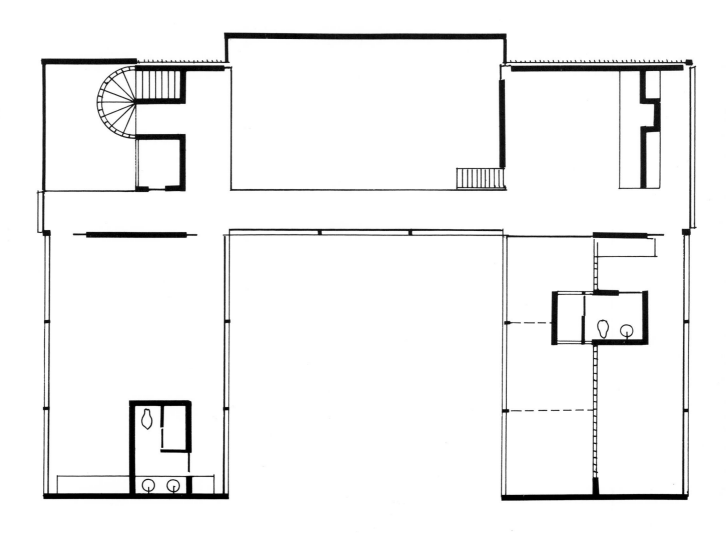

ACKNOWLEDGEMENTS

Northside Frame
Contractor—Crewe Construction Co.
Cabinets—Bolkuis Woodworking and Built-Ins

Suburban Italianate
None

Westside Vernacular
None

Greenhouse Kitchen
Architect for interior—Pier Bigongiari
Painting in living room—Robert Natkin
Painting in parlor—David McCullough

Landmark Restoration
Interior restoration—William L. Lavicka

Victorian Row House
Stained glass in kitchen—Andrea Lancer
Kitchen cabinets—Noelwood Handmade Furniture

Urban Mansion
None

Restored Romanesque
None

Towers and Turrets
None

Northside Gothic
Architect for interior—Bruno Ast with Gregory Tabb

Northside Revival
Architect for interior—Ralph Youngren

Southside Eclectic
Architect for kitchen remodeling—Harold Buttrich

Grande Dame
Paintings in living room—John Henry Vaughn

Renovated Storefront
Architect—James Kennedy
Contractor (Builders)—James and Thomas Kennedy

Prairie House
Interiors—Janet Schirn and Jo Fitch

Colonial Revival
None

Prairie Idiom
Painting in living room—David Sharpe

Chicago Tudor
Architect for remodeling—Herman Lackner
Interior design—Joseph Blake

Converted Garage
Interiors—Monika Betts
Architect—Bertram Berenson, Whitaker, Schroeder

Ex-urban Chateau
Landscape—Root and Hollister
Architect for room addition—Frank Polito

Georgian Manor
None

The Engineered House
None

The Wright Tradition
Watercolors—Edward Dart

Animal Crackers
Interior—Margaret McCurry
Painting in living room—Paul F. Pinzarrone
Black and white photos—Howard Kaplan

Sculptured Space
Architect—Laurence Booth, Booth and Hansen Associates
Contractor—Maddock Construction
Prints in study: Female figure—Artist, Jim Dine
                 Abstract print—Artist, Joan Miro
Painting in bedroom—Roger Brown

Glass House
Photos by Philip A. Turner and Sadin/Karant

For their generous and enthusiastic help, I would like to thank
Paul Caccia, Michael Johnson, Laurie Andrews, Ellen Benninghoven,
Jean Bloch, Laurence Booth, June Hill, Gary Husted, William Keck,
Mary Quinn-Olsson and Jeanne Sellegran. I am grateful to Stanley
Tigerman for his careful advice and to Jean Read for her guiding
intelligence. My warmest thanks go to Tom Dunne, author of the idea.